SP🕷t 7

7

SEEK & FIND

BY KIDSLABEL

Spooky

chronicle books·san francisco

The pairs of photos in this book of picture riddles seem the same...

but look carefully.
There are 7 differences.

You'll also find a **riddle** below each pair of photos.
Need a clue? The answer is always something
in the pictures above.

Extra Challenge
Looking only at the right-hand pages (and don't forget
the front cover!), find:

22 **bats**
3 **pocket watches**
3 **spoons**
3 **brooms**
2 **holes shaped like the number 7**
2 **bicycles**
2 **bunches of keys**

and a **tiger.**

A bunch of thieves were caught today:
They'd robbed a red-lined treasure chest—
they took the lining, they confessed,
but the stones they threw away.

The stones are gone, the thieves have dined,
and all that's left now is the _____!

Across my plain, dark and light armies clashed,
tossed and turned by distant hands.
Two monarchs overlooked this fight,
till cunning earned just one command.

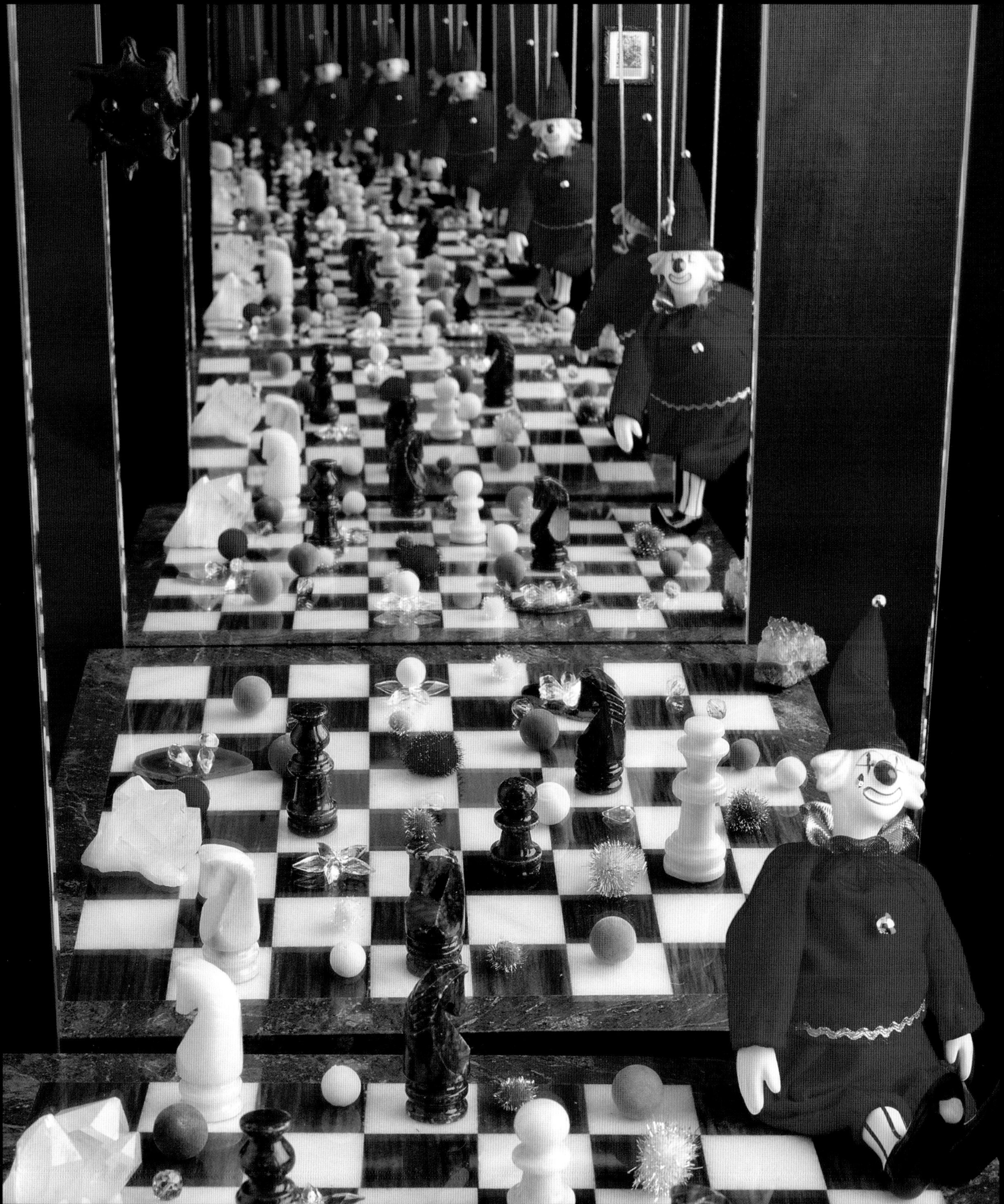

Disguised in sticks and shadows,
this slitherer's easily missed.
So don't trust your eyes, but listen
for the sound that's distinctively *hisss*.

This burning branch is stark and bare:
In a moment it splits the dark,
then where it was is only air.

Forgive me, my flame, if I wax poetic.
I burn only for you, but alas!
The closer you come, the more I melt away!

Round and white;
three dark holes;
teeth to bite;
but . . . no nose.

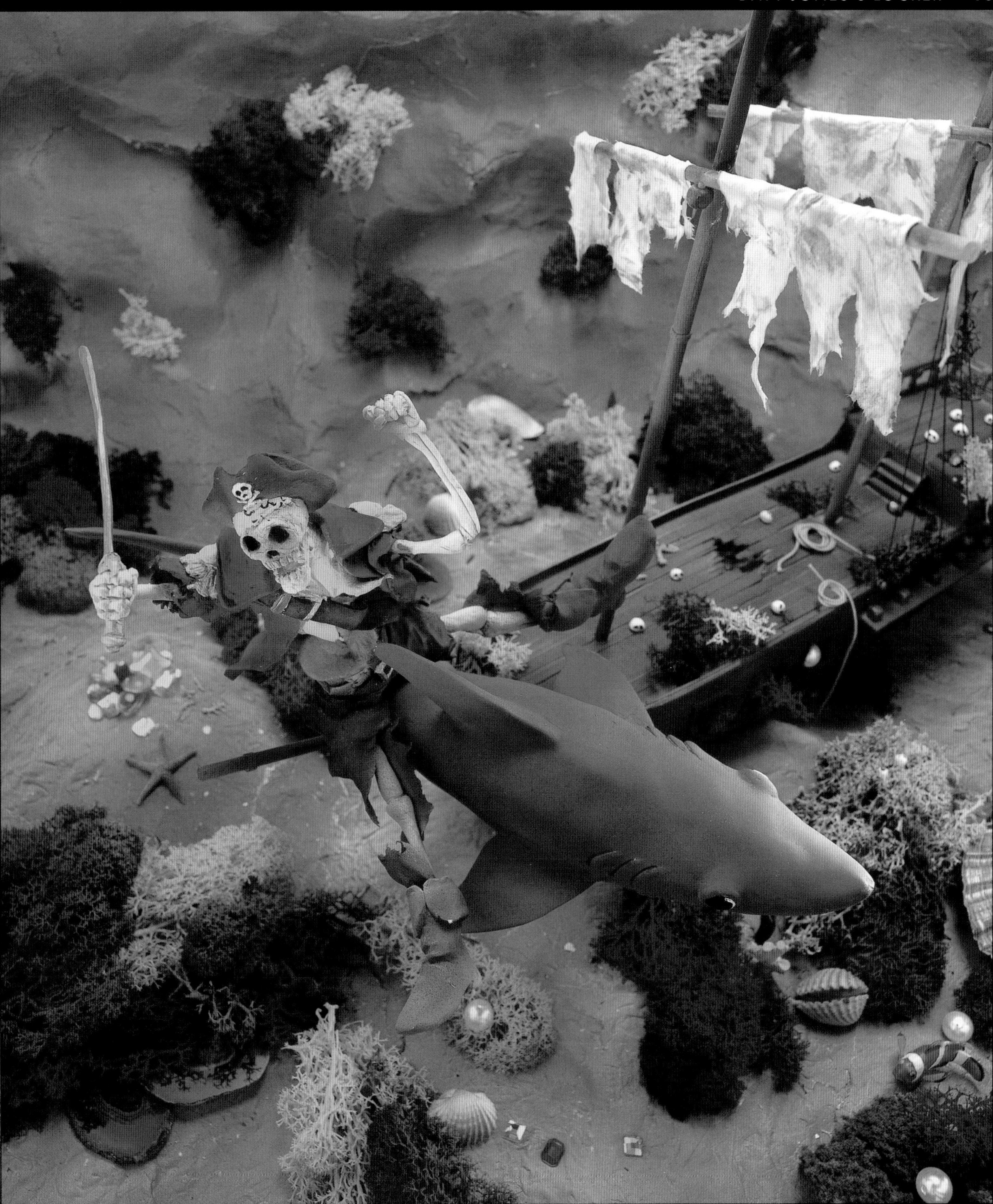

I can sit in the sun for hours,
but I won't turn brown.
Only when winter comes do I tan.
What am I?

Oh, when I am in, I am dazzling.
I shine so brightly I practically shout.
Oh, when I am in, I am dazzling,
but when I am dark, then I'm out.

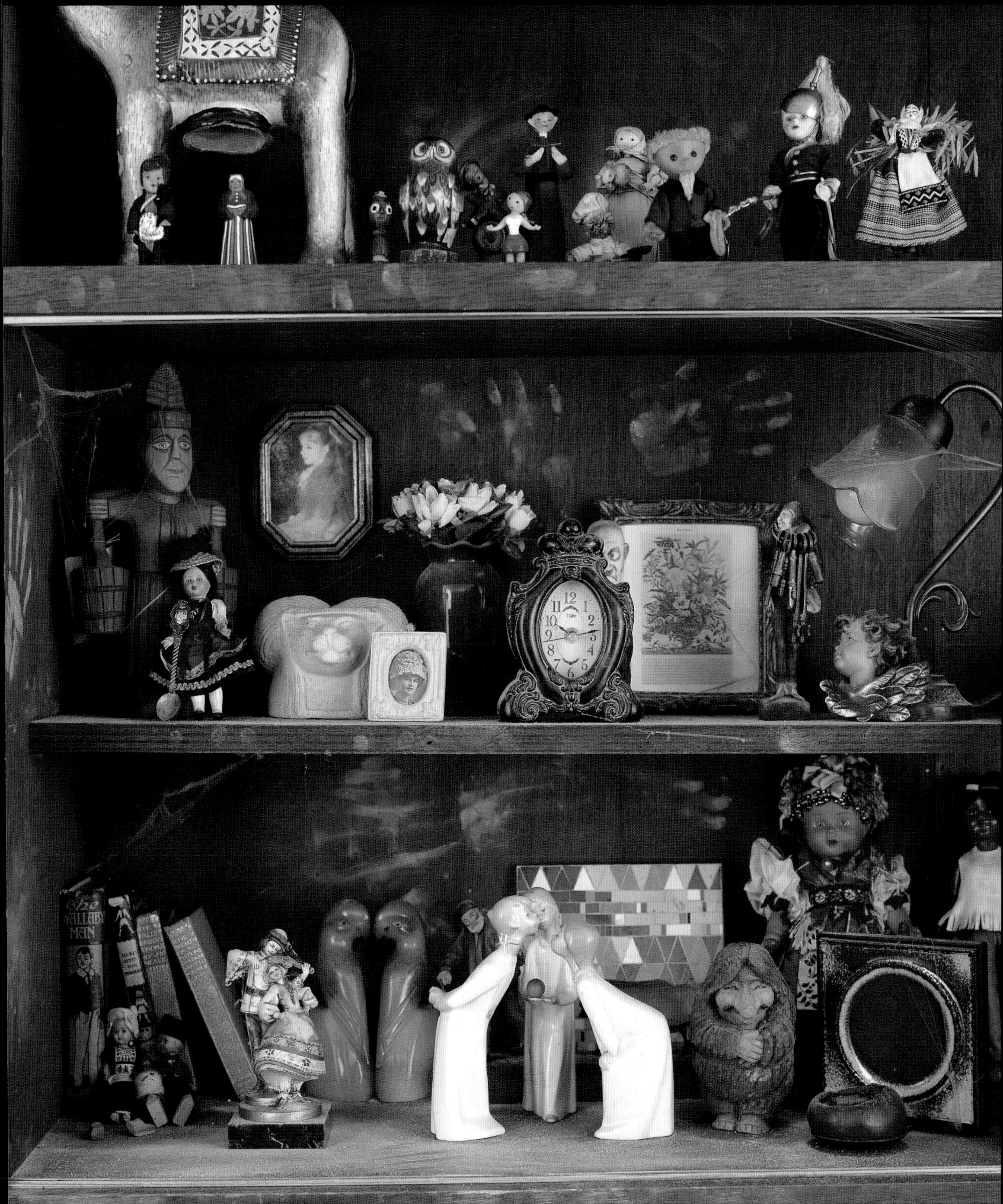
The WALLABY MAN

Watch out! In the living room you may meet
a thing with a back but not a chest;
arms but no hands; legs but no feet!

Bumping, thumping; rapping, tapping.
Sputter-spatter, rattle-patter; throb-bop, be-bop, BOOM!
I'm the tick-tock of music's clock,
and I may be small, but my voice needs ROOM!

(1) What do ghosts send home from vacation?
(2) What's a ghost's favorite treat?
(3) What amusement park ride do ghosts like best?

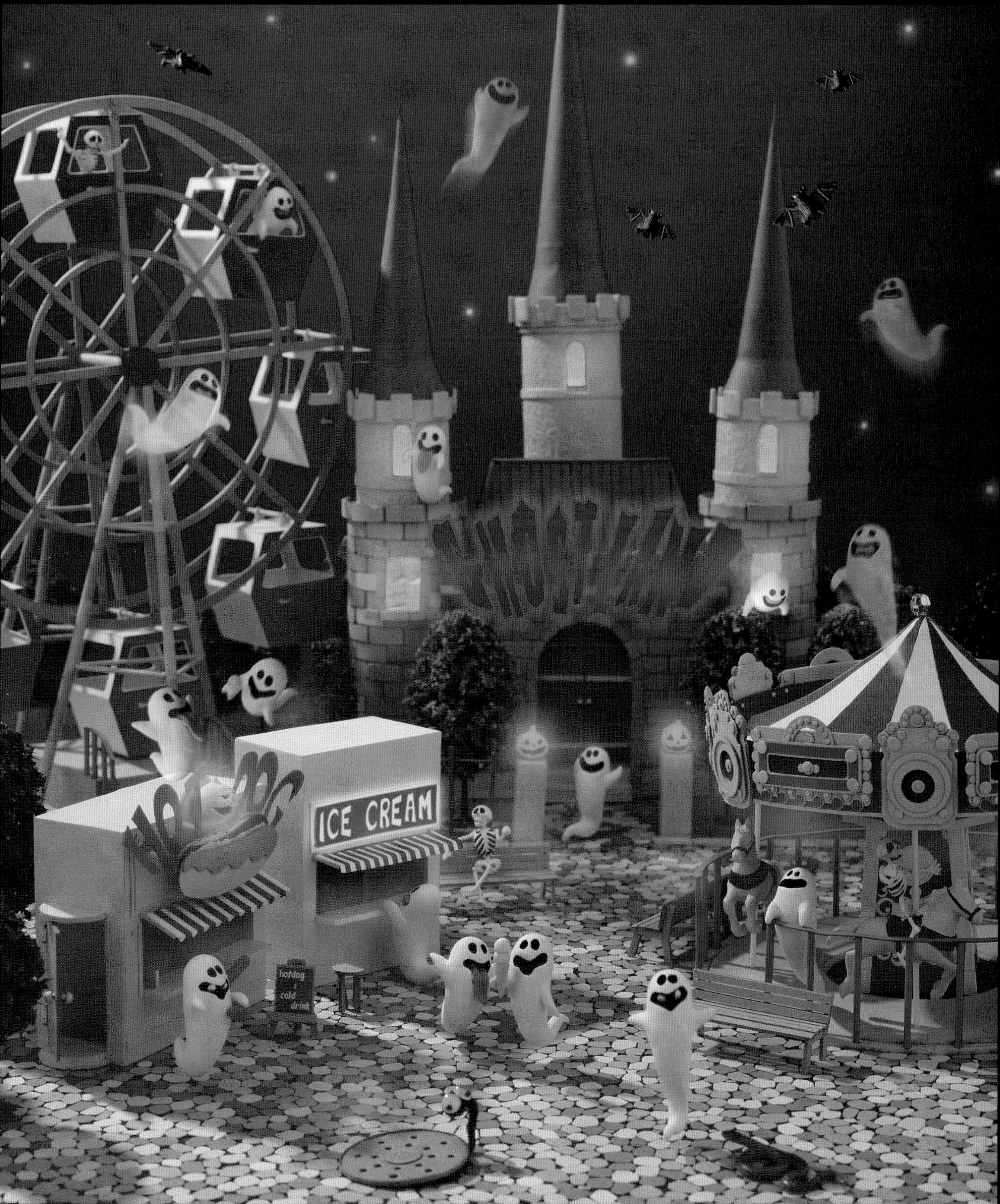
ICE CREAM
hotdog + cold drink

A rabbit buck went to a jeweler to buy a ring for the bunny he loved. "She said at least a carat," he told the ma
The man wrapped the ring up. "Take care, it's not returnable," he said. But the bunny left the jeweler without a
worry, and sniffed the aromatic air. Eternal love was just a gift away, or so he thought.

When the buck hare returned to his doe, she looked at the ring askance. "Take it back!" she said, fluffing her sleek hair. "Ritzy jewels are not for this humble rabbit!" "But what was it you wanted?" he asked her in confusion.

Alas, if the poor rabbit had been listening to this story, he would have heard the answer pronounced five times!

Front and Back Covers: Look for
a third footprint on a green stone
something shiny on a dinosaur's teeth
an ant on a white stone
a brown figure by the number 7
a red stone in a top corner
a green stone by a little face
a snake's head

Through the Black Hole: Look for
a treasure chest
a ship's flag
a watermelon
a television
a ring by a horse
a brown figure by a clock
an astronaut on a planet

The Hall of Mirrors: Look for
a painting on the wall
a green butterfly
a yellow pom-pom by a yellow ball
a black knight
a pawn that changes color
a white queen
a clown's tear

The Haunted Woods: Look for
a pale snake on a pale rock
a brown snake behind a tree
something green by a tree stump
a piece of leaf on a tree trunk
a stick near a yellow snake
something dark on a pink stone
a red stone behind a branch

Under a Bad Moon: Look for
a crystal by a pterodactyl skeleton
a pumpkin near the moon
a ghost on the left-hand side
a branch of lightning on the right
a butterfly near a path
a face on a tree
a lizard in the branches

Inside the Witch's House: Look for
a red lizard in a silver cup
a glass with red liquid
a candle flame
a ring in an hourglass
a card sticking out of a book
a stopper in a blue bottle
an apple with a face

Davy Jones's Locker: Look for
something yellow on the left-hand side
a starfish
a red jewel near the bottom
a clown fish near a corner
a skeleton's arm
something white on deck
a coil of rope

Behind the Dollhouse Door: Look for
a lizard on the screen
a light patch on a shadow
a doll lying down
a white figure by something red
something just above that
a ball on the wall
a figure's shadow

Ghostly Hands: Look for

a figure by an owl
a doll behind a doll with a beard
an angel's head
an extra book
a blue bead among three girls
an owl in a candle
something between two sitting dolls

Midnight: Look for

a shadow on the wall
a spoon on the floor
a train car that moves
a glass on the chair
a painting on the wall
a drawer
a cat's shadow

Eerie Masks: Look for

a yellow snake
a die on a pink flower
a little mask by a butterfly mask
a dark mask by a cat mask
something green on a frog mask
a bead in the eye of a blue demon
a black tooth

Ghosts on Vacation: Look for

an owl in a window
a ghost in another window
a shiny bead on a carousel
a skeleton riding a horse
a worm near a manhole
an open door
a skeleton on a bench

Food Bites Back: Look for

a green bell pepper
a refrigerator dial
an olive on a jar
a cork in a bottle
a straw in pink gelatin
a blueberry in a tomato
a part of the cap on an eggplant

Answers to the riddles:

Through the Black Hole: rind (watermelon)
The Hall of Mirrors: chessboard
The Haunted Woods: snake
Under a Bad Moon: lightning
Inside the Witch's House: candle
Davy Jones's Locker: skull
Behind the Dollhouse Door: leaf
Ghostly Hands: lightbulb
Midnight: chair
Eerie Masks: drum
Ghosts on Vacation:
(1) ghostcards (2) ice scream (3) the rollerghoster
Food Bites Back: carrot—if you read the story
aloud, you'll hear the word "carrot" in these
places:
least a **carat**," he
"Take **care, it**'s not
aromati**c air. Et**ernal
buc**k hare ret**urned
slee**k hair**. "**Rit**zy

Still can't find them?
Look at our Web page!
http://www.chroniclebooks.com/spot7

Spot some fun in
more!

available wherever books are sold!

Let's play
a counting game:
You hold me in your hands
and I will try to trip your feet.
For how many turns can you keep the beat?

sneak peek
**Spot 7
Animals**

First published in the United States in 2007 by Chronicle Books LLC.

Copyright © 2004 by KIDSLABEL Corp.
English text © 2007 by Chronicle Books LLC.
Originally published in Japan in 2004 under the title *Doko Doko Seven 4. Kowai!?* by KIDSLABEL Corp.
English translation rights arranged with KIDSLABEL Corp. through Japan Foreign-Rights Centre.
All rights reserved.

English type design by Meagan Bennett.
Typeset in Super Grotesk and Trade Gothic.
Manufactured in China.

Library of Congress Cataloging-in-Publication Data available.

Distributed in Canada by Raincoast Books
9050 Shaughnessy Street, Vancouver, British Columbia V6P 6E5

10 9 8 7 6 5 4 3 2 1

Chronicle Books LLC
680 Second Street, San Francisco, California 94107

www.chroniclekids.com

SPot 7